feeling SAD!

Published in paperback in 2019 by Wayland

Text copyright © Wayland 2017
Illustrations copyright © Mike Gordon 2017

Wayland
Carmelite House
50 Victoria Embankment
London EC4Y 0DZ

Wayland Australia
Level 17/207 Kent Street
Sydney, NSW 2000

Managing editor: Victoria Brooker
Creative design: Paul Cherrill

ISBN: 978 1 5263 0072 0

Printed in China

FSC
www.fsc.org

MIX
Paper from
responsible sources
FSC® C104740

Wayland is a division of
Hachette Children's Books,
an Hachette UK company.
www.hachette.co.uk

Feeling SAD!

Written by
Kay Barnham

Illustrated by
Mike Gordon

WAYLAND

Rio watched as Ethan kicked a
football against the school wall.
He looked really miserable.
"What's wrong with Ethan?"
Rio asked Jack.

"Haven't you heard?" said Jack.
"Ethan's moving house, which means he's moving
schools too. He's really upset about it."
"Oh dear," said Rio, who liked Ethan a lot.
He decided to try and cheer him up.

Next time the football headed in Rio's
direction, he kicked it back to Ethan.
"Hey," Rio said, "I hear you're leaving.
I'm sorry to hear that, mate."

"Not as sorry as I am," mumbled Ethan. And he booted the football so hard that it flew right over the school wall.

"Is there a football team at your new school?" asked Rio. Ethan brightened a little.
"I think so."
"That might be a good way to make friends," said Rio.

"Maybe," said Ethan. Then his face fell.
"What if I'm not good enough ...?"
"You're a *great* player!" said Rio.
"You bet!" said Ethan. He blushed.
"I'll just go and fetch the ball."

At lunchtime, Rio heard an odd noise in the library. He went to investigate and found Scarlett sniffing near the non-fiction books.

"What's up?" he said.

"My dog d-d-died," Scarlett replied.

And she put her face in her hands and wept.

"Oh dear," murmured Rio, who didn't know what to say. So he went to get the librarian.

The librarian came at once.

"Can I help, dear?" she asked Scarlett.

"No ..." Scarlett gulped back her tears.

"My dog died and I'm going to be sad for ever."

"I'm sorry to hear that," said the librarian.
"I once had a dog called Sonny.
When he died, I thought I'd never
stop crying." Scarlett looked up.
"So what happened next?" she said.

"Well," said the librarian, "first, I didn't want to talk about my dog at all. It made me feel too sad.

"But after a while, I thought about some of the really funny things Sonny used to do. Then I felt a little better."

"When he was a puppy, Buster used to wag his tail so hard that he fell over," said Scarlett, with the tiniest smile. Rio smiled too.

That afternoon, Mr Thomas read out the names for the school basketball team. "I don't believe it," Jordan muttered to Rio, when the PE teacher had finished speaking. "I'm not on the team." His face fell.

"Awww, Jordan," said Rio.
He knew how much his friend wanted to be a basketball player when he was older.
"That sucks."
"I might as well give up," Jordan said sadly.

Rio hated seeing his friend look so glum.
"*Don't* give up," he said to Jordan.
"Why not?" said Jordan. "If I haven't
been picked, then what's the point?"

"Rubbish," said Rio. "Look, why don't we go and speak to Mr Thomas and tell him how keen you are?"
"OK," grumbled Jordan.

"You're a really good player, Jordan,"
said Mr Thomas. "I just need you to work on
your dribbling and shooting skills before I can
put you in the team. Can you do that?"

Jordan beamed. "Of course," he said.
"I'm going to start *right* now."
And he gave Rio a high five.

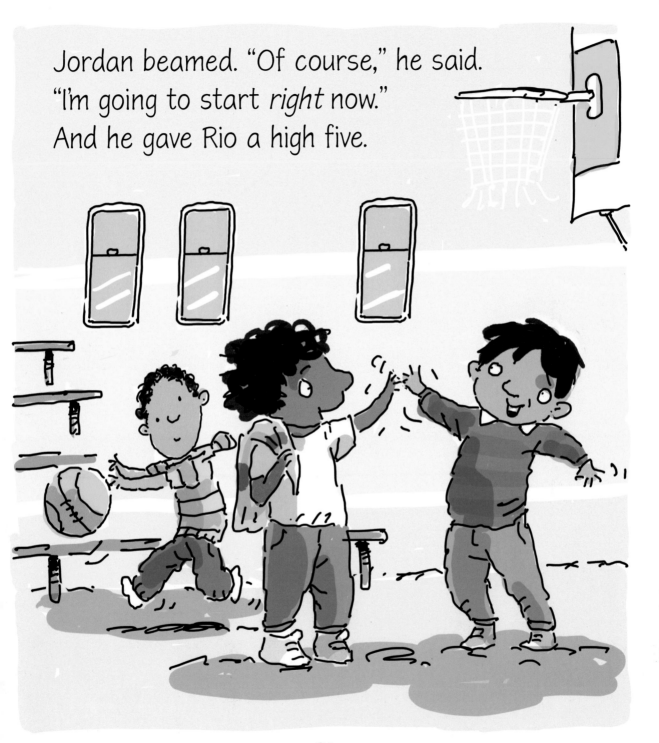

After school, Rio headed home.
He felt as if he'd been cheering people up all day.
But now it was his turn to feel sad. His dad was
working away from home and he really missed him.

"How many days is it now, Mum?"
he said at teatime.
"Fourteen," said his mum brightly.
"FOURTEEN?" Rio pulled a face.

"Cheer up," Mum said. "Dad will be home in just two weeks. That's hardly any time at all."
"That's *ages*," said Rio. "Why can't Dad work here, like everyone else's parents?"

"Sorry, love," said Mum.
"Dad's in construction. So he has to travel
to where the work is. And right now, the bridge
that he's building is a long way from home."
Rio knew all this. But it didn't make him
feel any better.

Thirteen days, twelve days, eleven days ... Rio couldn't believe how slowly time was passing. And still he felt sad.

Then he thought of Ethan and Scarlett and Jordan. If he could help them to feel happier, why couldn't he do the same for himself?

Rio knew that he couldn't make time go any faster, but he could keep himself busy. So he swam, he ran, he read, he hung out with friends and he played the guitar.

He visited his great-granny, who told him how his great-grandad went away during the war. And before he knew it, his dad was home.

"I missed you so much!" said Dad, giving Rio
a huge hug.

"Me too," said Rio. "I tried not to be too sad
while you were away, but I'm really happy that
you're back."

FURTHER INFORMATION

THINGS TO DO

1. Feeling sad sometimes makes people cry. So why not draw the outline of a big teardrop and fill it with as many happy things as you can. Perhaps next time you feel sad, this picture will make you feel happy instead.

2. This book shows lots of reasons why people might feel sad, such as moving house, the death of a pet, disappointing news or missing someone.

Can you think of any more reasons? Now can you think of ways to cheer someone up?

3. Make a colourful word cloud! Start with 'sad', then add any other words this makes you think of. Write them all down using different coloured pens. More important words should be bigger, less important words smaller. Start like this...

SAD $_{\text{Tears}}$ crying

NOTES FOR PARENTS AND TEACHERS

The aim of this book is to help children think about their feelings in an enjoyable, interactive way. Encourage them to have fun pointing to the illustrations, making sounds and acting, too. Here are more specific ideas for getting more out of this book:

1. Encourage children to talk about their own feelings, if they feel comfortable doing so, either while you are reading the book or afterwards. Here are some conversation prompts to try:

What makes you feel sad?
How do you stop feeling sad when this happens?

2. Make a facemask that shows a sad expression.

3. Put on a feelings play! Ask groups of children to act out the different scenarios in the book. The children could use their facemasks to show when they are sad in the play.

4. Hold a sad-face competition. Who can look the MOST sad?! Strictly no laughing allowed!

BOOKS TO SHARE

A Book of Feelings
by Amanda McCardie, illustrated by Salvatore Rubbino
(Walker, 2016)

The Secret Garden
by Frances Hodgson Burnett
(1905)

I Feel Sad
by Brian Moses, illustrated by Mike Gordon
(Wayland, 1994)

Michael Rosen's Sad Book
by Michael Rosen, illustrated by Quentin Blake
(Walker, 2011)

The Great Big Book of Feelings
by Mary Hoffman, illustrated by Ros Asquith
(Frances Lincoln, 2016)